D0963649

DO ONE THING EVERY DAY TOGETHER

▲
a journal for two
▼

by

♡ _____

and

♥ _____

INTRODUCTION

It takes two to tango, according to the 1952 song made popular by Pearl Bailey and Louis Armstrong. It also takes two to make a quarrel (eighteenth-century proverb), to make peace (John F. Kennedy), to be in a relationship, and to use *and* benefit from this book.

In *Do One Thing Every Day Together*, the two of you will have the chance to reflect on yourselves and your relationship by writing your own thoughts and sharing them with each other. You will be encouraged to record your ups and downs, similarities and differences, togetherness and "spaces in your togetherness" (Kahlil Gibran).

The year's worth of prompts in this book spring from the insights of writers and thinkers from biblical times to the present: poets, novelists, politicians, wits, philosophers, artists, and entertainers. Throughout the book are featured pages where you can compare yourselves with famous couples (Miss Bennet and Mr. Darcy, Beyoncé and Jay Z, Pooh and Piglet), find inspiration for the perfect small gift of love, remember firsts in your relationship, celebrate each other's admirable character traits, show off your intimate knowledge of each other, and compare likes and dislikes. You can also record themed "Together Days"—from listening to music to being in nature to doing nothing beyond spending the day together.

How does this work? First you write your names by the heart icons on the title page (either ♡ or ♥), which indicate the lines where you will record your responses. Then choose a convenient time to flip through the book together to a random page or a topic that fits your day. (Did you learn something new, enjoy the outdoors, have a fight and make up, or appreciate each other in some new or old way?) If you just can't find the right topic for both of you, use two different ones.

At the end of a year, when you have filled out and reread all the pages, you will have a deeper understanding not only of yourselves and of each other, but also of your relationship.

Are you ready to do this thing every day together, ♡ and ♥? Turn the page and begin.

DATE: ___/___/___

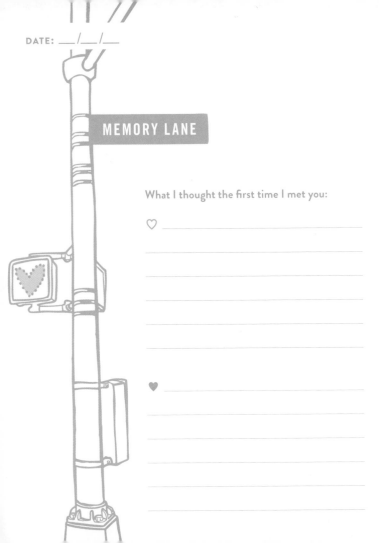

MEMORY LANE

What I thought the first time I met you:

♡ _____

_____

_____

_____

_____

_____

♥ _____

_____

_____

_____

_____

_____

They gave each other a smile with a future in it.

Ring Lardner

When I knew we had a future:

♡ _____

_____

_____

♥ _____

_____

_____

WITH A NAME LIKE YOURS, YOU MIGHT BE ANY SHAPE, ALMOST.

Lewis Carroll

When I first heard your name, I thought you would be:

♡ _____

_____

_____

♥ _____

_____

_____

What's in a name?
that which we call a rose
By any other name
would smell as sweet.

William Shakespeare

My pet name(s) for you:

♡ _____

_____

_____

♥ _____

_____

_____

There is only one happiness in life, to love and be loved.

George Sand

DATE: ___/___/___

HOW I SHOWED MY LOVE TODAY:

♡ _____

_____

♥ _____

_____

DATE: ___/___/___

WHAT MADE ME FEEL LOVED TODAY:

♡ _____

_____

♥ _____

_____

That is the happiest conversation where there is no competition, no vanity, but a calm, quiet interchange of sentiments.

Samuel Johnson

Today we had the happiest conversation about:

♡ _____

_____

♥ _____

_____

TOO MUCH AGREEMENT KILLS A CHAT.

Eldridge Cleaver

We had a good chat today, but we disagreed about:

♡ _____

_____

♥ _____

_____

DATE: ___/___/___

FAMOUS COUPLES
—

Miss Bennet

♥

Mr. Darcy

How do we compare?

♡ _____

_____

_____

♥ _____

_____

_____

DATE: ___/___/___

In vain have I struggled. It will not do. My feelings will not be repressed. You must allow me to tell you how ardently I admire and love you.

Jane Austen

Why I ardently admire and love you:

♡ _____

_____

_____

♥ _____

_____

_____

Where you used to be, there is a hole in the world, which I find myself constantly walking around in the daytime and falling into at night. I miss you like hell.

Edna St. Vincent Millay

Today when I missed you like hell, I:

♡ _____

_____

_____

♥ _____

_____

_____

ABSENCE DOTH SHARPEN LOVE, PRESENCE STRENGTHENS IT; THE ONE BRINGS FUEL, THE OTHER BLOWES IT TILL IT BURNES CLEARE.

Sir Thomas Overbury

How absence sharpened my love:

♡ _____

_____

_____

♥ _____

_____

_____

I SUPPOSE, THE FACT IS, THA
THE BREAKFAST TEST. . . . WH(
AMIABILITY FIRST THING IN

DATE: ___/___/___

My favorite time of day with you:

♡ _____

_____

_____

♥ _____

_____

_____

...NO FRIENDSHIP CAN STAND
...CAN BEGIN CONVENTIONAL
...THE MORNING? ◀ *Elizabeth von Arnim*

DATE: __/__/__

My least favorite time of day with you:

♡ _____

_____

_____

♥ _____

_____

_____

DATE: ___/___/___

HOW I FELL TODAY, AND YOU LIFTED ME UP:

♡ _____

_____

♥ _____

_____

DATE: ___/___/___

HOW YOU FELL TODAY, AND I LIFTED YOU UP:

♡ _____

_____

♥ _____

_____

TWO ARE BETTER THAN ONE. . . . FOR IF THEY FALL, THE ONE WILL LIFT UP HIS FELLOW.

Bible, Ecclesiastes

{ RICK }

HERE'S LOOKING AT YOU, KID.

Casablanca

The film star you remind me of:

♡ _____

_____

_____

♥ _____

_____

_____

DATE: ___/___/___

TOGETHER DAY

{ MOVIE }

The movie we saw together today:

_____

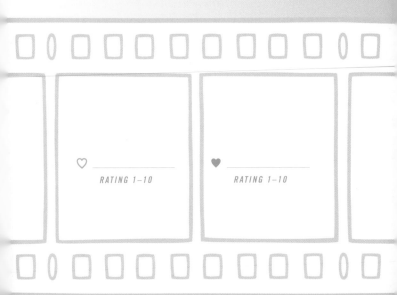

♡ _____
RATING 1–10

♥ _____
RATING 1–10

You should be kissed and often, and by someone who knows how.

Margaret Mitchell

Our most romantic kiss:

♡ _____

_____

_____

♥ _____

_____

_____

Sir, more than kisses, letters mingle souls.

John Donne

Your most romantic love note to me:

♡ _____

_____

_____

♥ _____

_____

_____

WHEN SOMEONE DOES SOMETHING WELL, APPLAUD! YOU WILL MAKE TWO PEOPLE HAPPY.

Samuel Goldwyn

DATE: ___/___/___

I APPLAUDED FOR YOU TODAY BECAUSE:

♡ _____

_____

♥ _____

_____

DATE: ___/___/___

YOU APPLAUDED FOR ME TODAY BECAUSE:

♡ _____

_____

♥ _____

_____

DATE: ___/___/___

IT TAKES
TWO TO MAKE
A QUARREL.

Proverb

What we quarreled about today:

♡ _____

_____

_____

♥ _____

_____

_____

It takes two to make peace.

John F. Kennedy

How we made peace today:

♡ _____

_____

_____

♥ _____

_____

_____

PERSONALITY RATING

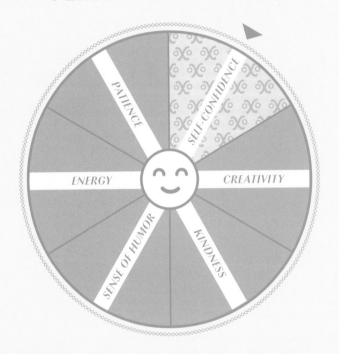

On a scale of 1 to 10, rate yourself and each other:

♡ ♥

♡ _____ ♥ _____

♥ _____ ♡ _____

Self-confidence is the first requisite to great undertakings.

Samuel Johnson

What I undertook with self-confidence today:

♡ _____

_____

_____

♥ _____

_____

_____

Everyone is a moon and has a dark side which he never shows to anybody.

Mark Twain

How your dark side showed today:

♡ _____

_____

_____

♥ _____

_____

IN YOUR LIGHT I
LEARN HOW TO LOVE.
IN YOUR BEAUTY,
HOW TO MAKE POEMS.

Rūmī

How your light inspired me today:

♡ _____

_____

_____

♥ _____

_____

_____

DATE: ___/___/___

YOUR KINDNESS TODAY:

♡ _____

_____

♥ _____

_____

DATE: ___/___/___

YOUR WHITE LIE TODAY:

♡ _____

_____

♥ _____

_____

In human relations kindness and lies are worth a thousand truths.

Graham Greene

To live is to change, and to be perfect is to have changed often.

John Henry Newman

How you have changed since we met:

♡ _____

_____

_____

♥ _____

_____

_____

Most women set out to try to change a man—and when they have changed him, they do not like him.

Marlene Dietrich

How I (fortunately) failed to change you:

♡ _____

_____

_____

♥ _____

_____

_____

DATE: ___/___/___

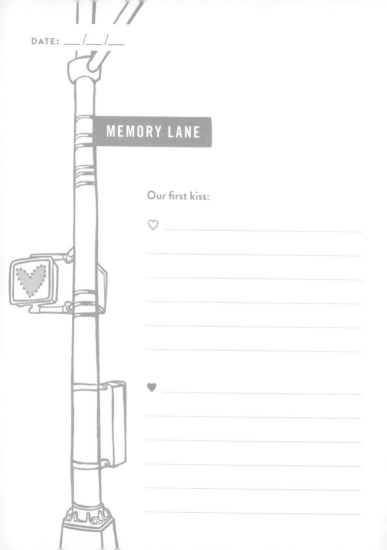

MEMORY LANE

Our first kiss:

♡ _____

_____

_____

_____

_____

_____

♥ _____

_____

_____

_____

_____

_____

A kiss can be a comma, a question mark or an exclamation point.

Mistinguette

The punctuation that marked our first kiss:

♡ _____

_____

_____

♥ _____

_____

_____

A gift is pure
when it is given
from the heart to the
right person at the
right time and at the
right place, and when
we expect nothing
in return.

Bhagavad Gita

DATE: ___/___/___

A GIFT I GAVE YOU FROM MY HEART TODAY:

♡ _____

_____

♥ _____

_____

DATE: ___/___/___

A GIFT I RECEIVED FROM YOUR HEART TODAY:

♡ _____

_____

♥ _____

_____

SPEAK WHEN YOU ARE ANGRY AND YOU WILL MAKE THE BEST SPEECH YOU WILL EVER REGRET.

Ambrose Bierce

What I regret saying to you today:

♡ _____

_____

_____

♥ _____

_____

_____

DATE: ___/___/___

The final form of love . . . is forgiveness.

Reinhold Niebuhr

Today I forgive you for:

♡ _____

_____

_____

♥ _____

_____

_____

ONE OF THE SECRETS OF A HAPPY LIFE IS CONTINUOUS SMALL TREATS.

Iris Murdoch

This small treat from you made me happy today:

♡ _____

_____

_____

♥ _____

_____

_____

DATE: ___/___/___

LOVE LETTERS

Place your stamp (♡ or ♥) on the message of love you delivered today.

flowers

a scented candle

tickets to a movie, show, or sporting event

a homemade gift

a love note in a secret spot

a tasty treat or homemade meal

a warm bubble bath

other

_____

DATE: ___/___/___

HOW WE SPENT TIME WITH OTHERS TODAY:

♡ _____

_____

♥ _____

_____

DATE: ___/___/___

WHAT WE ACCOMPLISHED TODAY:

♡ _____

_____

♥ _____

_____

BE NOT SOLITARY, BE NOT IDLE.

Robert Burton

Summer afternoon—
summer afternoon . . .
the two most beautiful
words in the English
language.

Henry James

The highlight of today's summer afternoon together:

♡ _____

_____

_____

♥ _____

_____

_____

OH, TO BE IN ENGLAND NOW THAT APRIL'S THERE.

Robert Browning

♡ Oh, to be in _____

_____

_____ .

♥ Oh, to be in _____

_____

_____ .

TOGETHER
DAY

{ COOKING }

The meal we cooked together today:

_____

♡ _____   ♥ _____

RATING 1–10   *RATING 1–10*

DATE: ___/___/___

ONE CANNOT THINK WELL, LOVE WELL, SLEEP WELL, IF ONE HAS NOT DINED WELL.

Virginia Woolf

Today we dined well, so I could:

♡ _____

_____

_____

♥ _____

_____

_____

I have spread my dreams
under your feet;
Tread softly because
you tread on my dreams.

William Butler Yeats

The dream I shared with you today:

♡ _____

_____

♥ _____

_____

_____

Dreaming permits each and every one of us to be quietly and safely insane every night of our lives.

Dr. William C. Dement

My insane dream last night:

♡ _____

_____

_____

♥ _____

_____

_____

JOY SHARED IS JOY DOUBLED; PAIN SHARED IS PAIN DIVIDED.

Friedrich Ruckert

DATE: ___/___/___

HOW WE DOUBLED A JOY TODAY:

♡ _____

_____

♥ _____

_____

DATE: ___/___/___

HOW WE DIVIDED A PAIN TODAY:

♡ _____

_____

♥ _____

_____

IT IS ONLY SHALLOW PEOPLE WHO DO NOT JUDGE BY APPEARANCES.

Oscar Wilde

What I liked best about your appearance today:

♡ _____

_____

_____

♥ _____

_____

_____

DATE: ___/___/___

A PLEASING COUNTENANCE IS NO SLIGHT ADVANTAGE.

Ovid

What you got away with today because you are so cute:

♡ _____

_____

_____

♥ _____

_____

_____

DATE: ___/___/___

THE BODY SAYS WHAT

♡ When you do this with your body: _____

      it means: _____

♥ When you do this with your body: _____

      it means: _____

DATE: __/__/__

WORDS CANNOT. ◀ **Martha Graham**

♡ When you do this with your hands: _____

it means: _____

♥ When you do this with your hands: _____

it means: _____

A friend is a person with whom I may be sincere. Before him, I may think aloud.

Ralph Waldo Emerson

I was thinking aloud today when I told you this:

♡ _____

_____

_____

♥ _____

_____

_____

WITH TRUE FRIENDS . . . EVEN WATER DRUNK TOGETHER IS SWEET ENOUGH.

Chinese proverb

How your friendship sweetened this dull day:

♡ _____

_____

_____

♥ _____

_____

_____

DATE: ___/___/___

PRAISE FOR ME FROM MYSELF TODAY:

♡ _____

_____

♥ _____

_____

DATE: ___/___/___

PRAISE FOR ME FROM YOU TODAY:

♡ _____

_____

♥ _____

_____

The advantage of doing one's praising for oneself is that one can lay it on so thick and exactly in the right places.

Samuel Butler

DATE: ___/___/___

TELL ME WHAT COMPANY THOU KEEPEST, AND I'LL TELL THEE WHAT THOU ART.

Miguel de Cervantes

Friends who bring out the best in you:

♡ _____

_____

_____

♥ _____

_____

_____

Have no friends not equal to yourself.

Confucius

Friends who are not equal to you:

♡ _____

_____

_____

♥ _____

_____

_____

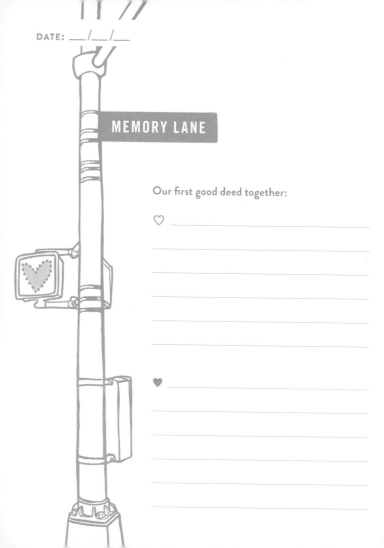

DATE: ___/___/___

MEMORY LANE

Our first good deed together:

♡ _____

_____

_____

_____

_____

♥ _____

_____

_____

_____

_____

I LOVE THEE FOR A HEART THAT'S KIND—
NOT FOR THE KNOWLEDGE IN THY MIND.

W. H. Davies

A kind gesture you made today:

♡ _____

_____

_____

♥ _____

_____

_____

DATE: ___/___/___

His socks compelled one's attention without losing one's respect.

Saki

What I love most about your fashion choices:

♡ _____

_____

_____

♥ _____

_____

_____

DATE: ___/___/___

Beauty when most unclothed is clothed best.

Phineas Fletcher

What I love most about your body:

♡ _____

_____

_____

♥ _____

_____

_____

To like
and dislike
the same
things, that is
indeed true
friendship.

Sallust

DATE: ___/___/___

WHAT WE BOTH LIKE:

♡ _____

_____

♥ _____

_____

DATE: ___/___/___

WHAT WE BOTH DISLIKE:

♡ _____

_____

♥ _____

_____

IT IS AS HEALTHY TO ENJOY SENTIMENT AS TO ENJOY JAM.

G. K. Chesterton

Why I got sentimental today:

♡ _____

_____

_____

♥ _____

_____

_____

I have a horror of sunsets, they're so romantic, so operatic.

Marcel Proust

Times when I do *not* feel romantic:

♡ _____

_____

_____

♥ _____

_____

_____

FAMOUS COUPLES
———

Macbeth ♥ Lady Macbeth

How do we compare?

♡ _____

_____

_____

♥ _____

_____

_____

DATE: ___/___/___

But screw your courage
to the sticking-place,
And we'll not fail.

William Shakespeare

How you gave me courage today:

♡ _____

_____

_____

♥ _____

_____

_____

A wise traveler never despises his own country.

Carlo Goldoni

Where we traveled in our own country today:

♡ _____

_____

_____

♥ _____

_____

_____

I am fevered with the sunset,
 I am fretful with the bay,
For the wander-thirst is on me
 And my soul is in Cathay.

Richard Hovey

Where we dreamed of traveling afar today:

♡ _____

_____

_____

♥ _____

_____

_____

TO SIT IN THE SHADE ON A
VERDURE IS THE MOST

DATE: __/__/__

My favorite outdoor activity with you:

♡ _____
_____
_____

♥ _____
_____
_____

...FINE DAY, AND LOOK UPON ...PERFECT REFRESHMENT. ◀ Jane Austen

DATE: __/__/__

My least favorite outdoor activity with you:

♡ _____

_____

_____

♥ _____

_____

_____

DATE: ___/___/___

HOW I WOULD CHANGE MYSELF:

♡ _____

_____

♥ _____

_____

DATE: ___/___/___

HOW I WOULD CHANGE YOU:

♡ _____

_____

♥ _____

_____

NEVER UNDERESTIMATE YOUR POWER TO CHANGE YOURSELF; NEVER OVERESTIMATE YOUR POWER TO CHANGE OTHERS.

H. Jackson Brown Jr.

DATE: ___/___/___

I hate housework! You make the beds, you do the dishes—and six months later you have to start all over again.

Joan Rivers

The household chore I hate most:

♡ _____

_____

_____

♥ _____

_____

_____

DATE: ___/___/___

TOGETHER DAY

{ HOUSEWORK }

The housework we

accomplished together today:

_____

How we made it tolerable:

 _____

♥ _____

TWO SOULS WITH BUT A SINGLE THOUGHT, TWO HEARTS THAT BEAT AS ONE.

Friedrich Halm

Our single thought today:

♡ _____

_____

_____

♥ _____

_____

_____

DATE: ___/___/___

The concept of two people living together for 25 years without having a cross word suggests a lack of spirit only to be admired in sheep.

A. P. Herbert

A cross word we had today:

♡ _____

_____

_____

♥ _____

_____

_____

"NO"
and "YES"
are words
quickly said,
but they need
a great amount
of thought
before you
utter them.

Baltasar Gracián

DATE: ___/___/___

WHY I SAID "NO" TO YOU TODAY:

♡ _____

_____

♥ _____

_____

DATE: ___/___/___

WHY I SAID "YES" TO YOU TODAY:

♡ _____

_____

♥ _____

_____

We could have saved sixpence. We have saved fivepence. [Pause] But at what cost?

Samuel Beckett

Money worth spending today:

♡ _____

_____

_____

♥ _____

_____

_____

MONEY IS LIKE MUCK, NOT GOOD EXCEPT IT BE SPREAD.

Sir Francis Bacon

Money I gave to a good cause today:

♡ _____

_____

_____

♥ _____

_____

_____

DATE: __/__/__

PERSONALITY RATING

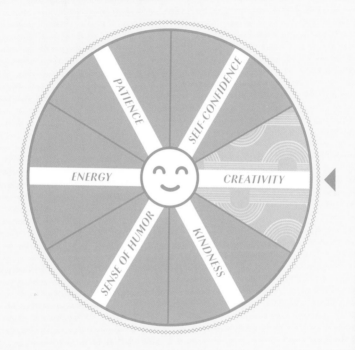

On a scale of 1 to 10, rate yourself and each other:

♡

♡ _____   ♥ _____

♥ _____   ♡ _____

In order to create there must be a dynamic force, and what force is more potent than love?

Igor Stravinsky

How you inspired me to be creative today:

♡ _____

_____

_____

♥ _____

_____

_____

ONE KIND WORD CAN WARM THREE WINTER MONTHS.

Japanese proverb

The kind word you warmed me with today:

♡ _____

_____

_____

♥ _____

_____

_____

{ PRINCESS LEIA }

Why, you stuck-up . . . half-witted . . . scruffy-looking . . . nerf herder!

The Empire Strikes Back

Unkind words I wish I hadn't said today:

♡ _____

_____

_____

♥ _____

_____

_____

DATE: ___ / ___ / ___

WHAT MADE ME A LITTLE LARGER TODAY:

♡ _____

_____

♥ _____

_____

DATE: ___ / ___ / ___

WHAT MADE ME A LITTLE SMALLER TODAY:

♡ _____

_____

♥ _____

_____

A single day
is enough to
make us a little
larger or, another
time, a little
smaller.

Paul Klee

Love is made by two people, in different kinds of solitude.

Louis Aragon

What I did in my solitude today:

♡ _____

_____

_____

♥ _____

_____

_____

Love does not consist in gazing at each other, but in looking together in the same direction.

Antoine de Saint-Exupéry

The direction where we both looked today:

♡ _____

_____

_____

♥ _____

_____

_____

DATE: ___/___/___

MEMORY LANE

How I felt at our first party as a couple:

♡ _____

_____

_____

_____

_____

♥ _____

_____

_____

_____

_____

I entertained on a cruising trip that was so much fun that I had to sink my yacht to make the guests go home.

F. Scott Fitzgerald

Best. Party. Ever.

♡ _____

_____

_____

♥ _____

_____

_____

HE WHO HAS NOT AN ADVENTURE HAS NOT HORSE OR MULE.... [HE] WHO IS TOO ADVENTUROUS ... LOSES HORSE AND MULE.

François Rabelais

DATE: ___/___/___

WHEN WE ADVENTURED TOO LITTLE:

♡ _____

_____

♥ _____

_____

DATE: ___/___/___

WHEN WE ADVENTURED TOO MUCH:

♡ _____

_____

♥ _____

_____

DATE: ___/___/___

DO NOT THE MOST MOVING MOMENTS OF OUR LIVES FIND US ALL WITHOUT WORDS?

Marcel Marceau

Why I was without words today:

♡ _____

_____

_____

♥ _____

_____

_____

Dumb swans, not chattering pies, do lovers prove;
They love indeed who quake to say they love.

Sir Philip Sidney

When you finally told me you loved me:

♡ _____

_____

_____

♥ _____

_____

_____

DATE: ___/___/___

Who hath not saved some trifling thing
More prized than jewels rare,
A faded flower, a broken ring,
A tress of golden hair.

Ellen C. Howarth

A "trifling" gift from you that I prize:

♡ _____

_____

_____

♥ _____

_____

_____

LOVE LETTERS

Place your stamp (♡ or ♥) on the message of love you delivered today.

Often . . . our own light goes out, and is rekindled by some experience we go through with a fellow man.

Albert Schweitzer

How you rekindled my light today:

♡ _____

_____

_____

♥ _____

_____

_____

THEN COME THE WILD WEATHER, COME SLEET OR COME SNOW, WE WILL STAND BY EACH OTHER, HOWEVER IT BLOW.

Simon Dach

How you stood by me today:

♡ _____

_____

_____

♥ _____

_____

_____

I HAVE ONLY
GOT DOWN ON
TO PAPER, REALLY,
THREE TYPES
OF PEOPLE:
THE PERSON I THINK
I AM, THE PEOPLE WHO
IRRITATE ME, AND THE
PEOPLE I'D LIKE TO BE.

E. M. Forster

DATE: ___/___/___

THE PERSON I THINK I AM:

♡ _____

♥ _____

DATE: ___/___/___

PEOPLE WHO IRRITATE ME:

♡ _____

♥ _____

DATE: ___/___/___

PEOPLE I'D LIKE TO BE:

♡ _____

♥ _____

DATE: __/__/__

THERE ARE THREE SIDES TO EVERY ARGUMENT: YOUR SIDE, MY SIDE, AND THE TRUTH.

American proverb

Our argument today:

♡ MY SIDE: _____   ♡ MY SIDE: _____

_____   _____

_____   _____

_____   _____

♡ ♥ THE TRUTH:

_____

_____

DATE: ___/___/___

So I have talked with Betsey, and

Betsey has talked with me,

And so we've agreed together that

we can't never agree.

Will Carleton

What we agreed to disagree about today:

♡ _____

_____

_____

♥ _____

_____

_____

TOGETHER DAY

{ MUSIC }

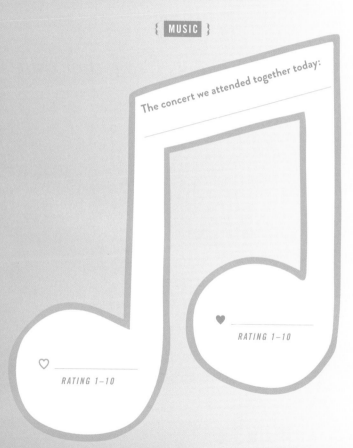

The concert we attended together today: ___

♡ ___

RATING 1–10

♥ ___

RATING 1–10

Music washes away from the soul the dust of everyday life.

▲

Berthold Auerbach

▼

Music that washed the dust away today:

♡ _____

_____

_____

♥ _____

_____

_____

I CAN NEITHER EAT NOR SLEEP FOR THINKING OF YOU MY DEAREST LOVE, I NEVER TOUCH EVEN PUDDING.

Horatio, Lord Nelson

All the times I thought about you today:

♡ _____

_____

_____

♥ _____

_____

_____

How do I love thee? Let me count the ways.

Elizabeth Barrett Browning

♡

1. _____

2. _____

3. _____

4. _____

5. _____

♥

1. _____

2. _____

3. _____

4. _____

5. _____

It ain't bragging if you can do it.

Dizzy Dean

DATE: ___/___/___

WHAT I CAN DO:

♡ _____

_____

♥ _____

_____

DATE: ___/___/___

WHAT YOU CAN DO:

♡ _____

_____

♥ _____

_____

DATE: ___/___/___

HE IS THE VERY PINEAPPLE OF POLITENESS!

Richard Brinsley Sheridan

♡ You are the very _____ of politeness.

♥ You are the very _____ of politeness.

DATE: ___/___/___

It is an immense loss to have all robust and sustaining expletives refined away from one; at such moments of trial refinement is a feeble reed to lean upon.

Alice James

My favorite expletive:

♡ _____

_____

_____

♥ _____

_____

_____

DATE: ___/___/___

WHEN SHE RAISES HE
WERE TAKING OF

♡ When you do this with your eyes: _____

     it means: _____

♥ When you do this with your eyes: _____

     it means: _____

DATE: ___/___/___

EYELIDS IT'S AS IF SHE
ALL HER CLOTHES. ◀ Colette

♡ When you do this with your eyebrows: _____

      it means: _____

♥ When you do this with your eyebrows: _____

      it means: _____

DATE: __/__/__

COME. LET'S HAVE ONE OTHER GAUDY NIGHT....LET'S MOCK THE MIDNIGHT BELL.

William Shakespeare

Our gaudy night:

♡ _____

_____

_____

♥ _____

_____

_____

DATE: ___/___/___

WHOEVER THINKS OF GOING TO BED BEFORE TWELVE O'CLOCK IS A SCOUNDREL.

Samuel Johnson

What we did after midnight last night:

♡ _____

_____

_____

♥ _____

_____

_____

What is most beautiful in virile men is something feminine; what is most beautiful in feminine women is something masculine.

Susan Sontag

DATE: ___/___/___

SOMETHING BEAUTIFULLY FEMININE ABOUT YOU:

♡ _____

_____

♥ _____

_____

DATE: ___/___/___

SOMETHING BEAUTIFULLY MASCULINE ABOUT YOU:

♡ _____

_____

♥ _____

_____

EVERYTHING YOU SEE I OWE TO SPAGHETTI.

Sophia Loren

♡ Everything you see I owe to _____ .

♥ Everything you see I owe to _____ .

I am glad that my Adonis hath a sweete tooth in his head.

John Lyly

How I indulged your sweet tooth today:

♡ _____

_____

_____

♥ _____

_____

_____

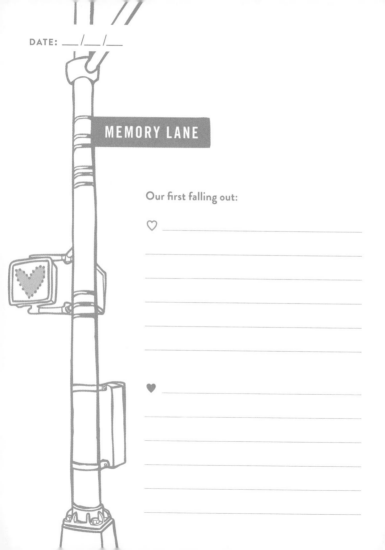

DATE: ___/___/___

MEMORY LANE

Our first falling out:

♡ _____

_____

_____

_____

_____

_____

♥ _____

_____

_____

_____

_____

_____

DATE: ___ / ___ / ___

And blessings on the falling out
That all the more endears,
When we fall out with those we love
And kiss again with tears!

Alfred, Lord Tennyson

How we made up today:

♡ _____

_____

_____

♥ _____

_____

_____

DATE: ___/___/___

Of all the days, the day on which one has not laughed is the one most surely wasted.

▲
▼

Sébastien-Roch Nicolas de Chamfort

Today we laughed about:

♡ _____

_____

_____

♥ _____

_____

_____

ANYONE CAN BE PASSIONATE, BUT IT TAKES REAL LOVERS TO BE SILLY.

Rose Franken

Today we were silly about:

♡ _____

_____

_____

♥ _____

_____

_____

*TODAY WELL LIVED
MAKES EVERY
YESTERDAY A DREAM
OF HAPPINESS, AND
EVERY TOMORROW
A VISION OF HOPE.
LOOK WELL
THEREFORE TO THIS
DAY!*

Salutation of the Dawn (Sanscrit)

DATE: ___/___/___

HOW I LIVED WELL TODAY:

♡ _____

_____

♥ _____

_____

DATE: ___/___/___

HOW I HOPE TO LIVE WELL TOMORROW:

♡ _____

_____

♥ _____

_____

If you listen long enough—
or is it deep enough?—the
silence of a lover can speak
plainer than any words!

Phyllis Bottome

What your silence said to me today:

♡ _____

_____

_____

♥ _____

_____

_____

A comfortable quiet had settled between them. A silence that was like newly fallen snow.

Carrie Fisher

Today's comfortable silence:

♡ _____

_____

_____

♥ _____

_____

_____

DATE: ___/___/___

Jay Z

♥

Beyoncé

How do we compare?

♡ _____

_____

_____

♥ _____

_____

_____

DATE: ___/___/___

I'LL BE THERE FOR YOU,
IF SOMEBODY HURTS YOU
EVEN IF THAT
SOMEBODY'S ME.

Beyoncé, in Jay Z's "Bonnie & Clyde"

How you were there for me today:

♡ _____

_____

_____

♥ _____

_____

_____

FAMILIAR ACTS ARE BEAUTIFUL THROUGH LOVE.

Percy Bysshe Shelley

A familiar act made beautiful because we did it together today:

♡ _____

_____

_____

♥ _____

_____

_____

FAMILIARITY BREEDS CONTENT.

Anna Quindlen

When we felt contented together today:

♡ _____

_____

_____

♥ _____

_____

_____

I LOVE CITY LIFE. ALL THE
SEE IN COUNTRY LIFE, I FIND
THE MULTITUDES OF PEOPLE.

DATE: __/__/__

My favorite city activity with you:

♡ _____
_____
_____
♥ _____
_____
_____

BEAUTY THAT OTHER PEOPLE
TAKING WALKS AND SEEING

◀ Ezra Jack Keats

DATE: ___/___/___

My least favorite city activity with you:

♡ _____

_____

_____

♥ _____

_____

_____

All the art
of living lies
in a fine
mingling
of letting
go and
holding on.

Havelock Ellis

DATE: ___/___/___

HOW I LET GO OF YOU TODAY:

♡ _____

_____

♥ _____

_____

DATE: ___/___/___

HOW I HELD ON TO YOU TODAY:

♡ _____

_____

♥ _____

_____

TOGETHER DAY

{ SPORTS }

The sport we played together today:

_____

♡ _____
RATING 1–10

♥ _____
RATING 1–10

Sports do not build character. They reveal it.

Heywood Hale Broun

What sports revealed to me about your character today:

♡ _____

_____

_____

♥ _____

_____

_____

Whatever souls are made of, his and mine are the same.

Emily Brontë

How our souls were the same today:

♡ _____

_____

_____

♥ _____

_____

_____

"Let us agree not to step on each other's feet," said the cock to the horse.

English proverb

How I kept out of your way today:

♡ _____

_____

_____

♥ _____

_____

_____

Service is the rent that you pay for room on this earth.

Shirley Chisholm

DATE: ___ /___ /___

MY SERVICE TO MY COMMUNITY TODAY:

♡ _____

_____

♥ _____

_____

DATE: ___ /___ /___

MY SERVICE TO MY COUNTRY TODAY:

♡ _____

_____

♥ _____

_____

PURSUIT AND SEDUCTION ARE THE ESSENCE OF SEXUALITY. IT'S PART OF THE SIZZLE.

Camille Paglia

When we sizzled today:

♡ _____

_____

_____

♥ _____

_____

_____

The deep, deep peace of the double-bed after the hurly-burly of the chaise-longue.

Mrs. Patrick Campbell

The deep, deep peace of being in a relationship with you:

♡ _____

_____

_____

♥ _____

_____

_____

PERSONALITY RATING

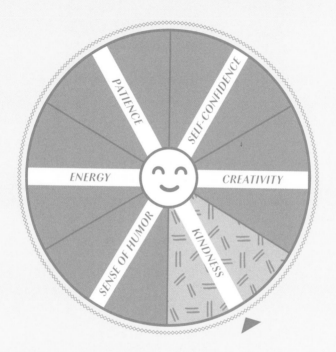

On a scale of 1 to 10, rate yourself and each other:

♡

♡ _____

♥ _____

♥

♥ _____

♡ _____

Shall we make a new rule of life from to-night: always to try to be a little kinder than is necessary?

J. M. Barrie

How I will be kinder than necessary to you tomorrow:

♡ _____

_____

_____

♥ _____

_____

_____

WHEN YOU HUG SOMEONE, YOU LEARN SOMETHING ELSE ABOUT THEM. AN IMPORTANT SOMETHING ELSE.

E. L. Konigsburg

What I learned from our hug today:

♡ _____

_____

_____

♥ _____

_____

_____

DATE: ___/___/___

A kiss . . . 'tis a secret
Told to the mouth
instead of to the ear.

Edmond Rostand

The secret you told to my mouth today:

♡ _____

_____

_____

♥ _____

_____

_____

DATE: ___/___/___

YOUR DEPLORABLE EXTRAVAGANCE TODAY:

♡ _____

_____

♥ _____

_____

DATE: ___/___/___

MY REASONABLE EXTRAVAGANCE TODAY:

♡ _____

_____

♥ _____

_____

WE BOTH
DEPLORE
EXTRAVAGANCE.
HE DEPLORES
MINE, AND I
DEPLORE HIS.

Jane Goodsell

The accent of one's birthplace remains in the mind and in the heart as in one's speech.

François de La Rochefoucauld

What I heard in your words that reflected your birthplace today:

♡ _____

_____

_____

♥ _____

_____

_____

NATURE IS OFTEN HIDDEN, SOMETIMES OVERCOME; SELDOM EXTINGUISHED.

Sir Francis Bacon

My inextinguishable nature, which showed itself today:

♡ _____

_____

_____

♥ _____

_____

_____

DATE: ___/___/___

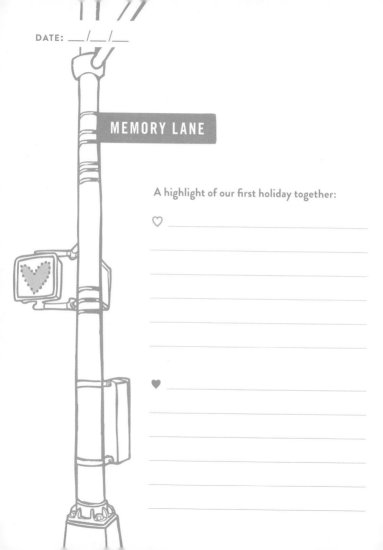

MEMORY LANE

A highlight of our first holiday together:

♡ _____

_____

_____

_____

_____

_____

♥ _____

_____

_____

_____

_____

Come, woo me, woo me; for now I am in a holiday humor, and like enough to consent.

William Shakespeare

A romantic holiday moment today:

♡ _____

_____

_____

♥ _____

_____

_____

Friendship
is a strong and
habitual inclination
in two persons to
promote the good
and happiness of
one another.

Eustace Budgell

DATE: ___/___/___

HOW YOU PROMOTED MY GOOD TODAY:

♡ _____

_____

♥ _____

_____

DATE: ___/___/___

HOW YOU PROMOTED MY HAPPINESS TODAY:

♡ _____

_____

♥ _____

_____

HIS VERY FAULTS SMACK OF THE RACINESS OF HIS GOOD QUALITIES.

Washington Irving

Your faults that are actually virtues:

♡ _____

_____

_____

♥ _____

_____

_____

When the defects of others are perceived with so much clarity, it is because one possesses them oneself.

Jules Renard

Defects we share:

♡ _____

_____

_____

♥ _____

_____

_____

DATE: ___/___/___

No possession is gratifying without a companion.

Seneca

The possession that gratified both of us today:

♡ _____

_____

_____

♥ _____

_____

_____

LOVE LETTERS

Place your stamp (♡ or ♥) on the message of love you delivered today.

flowers

a scented candle

tickets to a movie, show, or sporting event

a homemade gift

a love note in a secret spot

a tasty treat or homemade meal

a warm bubble bath

other

_____

Constant togetherness is fine—but only for Siamese twins.

Victoria Billings

What we did separately today:

♡ _____

_____

_____

♥ _____

_____

_____

DATE: ___/___/___

All who joy would win Must share it, happiness was born a twin.

Lord Byron

Happiness we shared today:

♡ _____

_____

_____

♥ _____

_____

_____

DATE: ___/___/___

MY BOILING POINT:

♡ _____

_____

♥ _____

_____

DATE: ___/___/___

YOUR BOILING POINT:

♡ _____

_____

♥ _____

_____

WE BOIL AT DIFFERENT DEGREES.

Ralph Waldo Emerson

THE BEST THINGS IN LIFE ARE NOT THINGS.

Proverb

The best thing in life today:

♡ _____

_____

_____

♥ _____

_____

_____

DATE: ___/___/___

WE LOOK TOO MUCH TO MUSEUMS. THE SUN COMING UP IN THE MORNING IS ENOUGH.

Romare Bearden

The best thing in nature today:

♡ _____

_____

_____

♥ _____

_____

_____

DATE: __/__/__

TOGETHER DAY

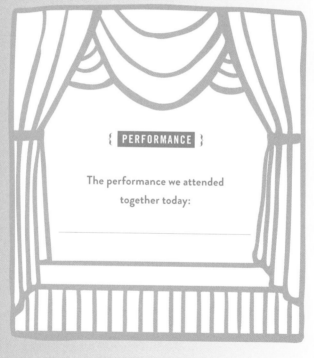

{ **PERFORMANCE** }

The performance we attended
together today:

_____

♡ _____ ♥ _____

RATING 1–10   *RATING 1–10*

I find that people's eyes can be opened as well from the stage as from a pulpit.

Henrik Ibsen

What we saw on stage today that opened my eyes:

♡ _____

_____

_____

♥ _____

_____

_____

Only passions, great passions, can elevate the soul to great things.

Denis Diderot

My great passion:

♡ _____

_____

_____

♥ _____

_____

_____

DATE: ___/___/___

NOT TOO MUCH ENTHUSIASM.

Charles-Maurice de Talleyrand

▲
▼

Why we restrained our enthusiasm today:

♡ _____

_____

_____

♥ _____

_____

_____

WHEN
I'M GOOD,
I'M VERY GOOD,
BUT WHEN
I'M BAD,
I'M BETTER.

Mae West

DATE: ___/___/___

HOW I WAS GOOD (VERY GOOD) TODAY:

♡ _____

_____

♥ _____

_____

DATE: ___/___/___

HOW I WAS BAD (BETTER) TODAY:

♡ _____

_____

♥ _____

_____

DATE: ___/___/___

Jack Sprat
Could eat no Fat,
His Wife could eat no Lean;
And so, betwixt them both,
They lick'd the Platter clean.

Mother Goose

How we complemented each other today:

♡ _____

_____

_____

♥ _____

_____

_____

IT'S OUR *OWN* STORY EXACTLY! HE BOLD AS A HAWK, SHE SOFT AS THE DAWN.

James Thurber

Our own story:

♡

I am _____ as a _____ .

You are _____ as a _____ .

♥

I am _____ as a _____ .

You are _____ as a _____ .

DATE: ___/___/___

"WHEN I USE A WORD, IN A RATHER SCORNFUL TON IT TO MEAN—NEITHE

♡ When you say this: _____

      it means: _____

♥ When you say this: _____

      it means: _____

DATE: ___/___/___

HUMPTY DUMPTY SAID,
IT MEANS JUST WHAT I CHOOSE
MORE NOR LESS." ◀ **Lewis Carroll**

♡ When you don't say this: _____

      it means: _____

♥ When you don't say this: _____

      it means: _____

GOOD COMPANY IN A JOURNEY MAKES THE WAY TO SEEM THE SHORTER.

Izaak Walton

How you made a long journey seem shorter today:

♡ _____

_____

_____

♥ _____

_____

_____

Separate from the pleasure of your company, I don't much care if I never see another mountain in my life.

Charles Lamb

♡ Separate from your company, I don't care if I never see another

_____ in my life.

♥ Separate from your company, I don't care if I never see another

_____ in my life.

DATE: ___/___/___

GLADNESS WE SHARED TODAY:

♡ _____

_____

♥ _____

_____

DATE: ___/___/___

TEARS WE WEPT TOGETHER TODAY:

♡ _____

_____

♥ _____

_____

WE HAVE LIVED AND
LOVED TOGETHER
THROUGH MANY
CHANGING YEARS,
WE HAVE SHARED EACH
OTHER'S GLADNESS,
AND WEPT EACH
OTHER'S TEARS.

Charles Jefferys

I AM TWO FOOLS, I KNOW, FOR LOVING, AND FOR SAYING SO IN WHINING POETRY.

John Donne

Write a loving couplet to each other:

♡ _____

_____

♥ _____

_____

I court others in verse; but I love thee in prose:
And they have my whimsies, but thou hast my heart.

Matthew Prior

Write a loving sentence to each other:

♡ _____

_____

_____

♥ _____

_____

_____

MEMORY LANE

A highlight from the first time I met your family:

♡ _____

_____

_____

_____

_____

♥ _____

_____

_____

_____

_____

DATE: ___/___/___

HAPPINESS IS HAVING A LARGE, LOVING, CARING, CLOSE–KNIT FAMILY IN ANOTHER CITY.

George Burns

My favorite members of your family:

♡ _____

_____

_____

♥ _____

_____

_____

The test of pleasure is the memory it leaves behind.

Jean Paul Richter

The memory our pleasure today left behind:

♡ _____

_____

_____

♥ _____

_____

_____

The sense of smell, almost more than any other, has the power to recall memories.

Rachel Carson

The scent that recalled a memory of you today:

♡ _____

_____

_____

♥ _____

_____

_____

*I love
her too,
but our
neuroses
just don't
match.*

Arthur Miller

DATE: ___/___/___

OUR NEUROSES MATCHED TODAY:

♡ _____

_____

♥ _____

_____

DATE: ___/___/___

OUR NEUROSES DIDN'T MATCH TODAY:

♡ _____

_____

♥ _____

_____

{ OLIVER HARDY }

Here's another nice mess you've gotten me into.

▲

The Laurel-Hardy Murder Case

▼

A mess you got me into today:

♡ _____

_____

_____

♥ _____

_____

_____

HOUSTON, WE'VE HAD A PROBLEM.

James Lovell

A mess you got me out of today:

♡ _____

_____

_____

♥ _____

_____

_____

FAMOUS COUPLES
_____

Pooh
♥
Piglet

How do we compare?

♡ _____

_____

_____

♥ _____

_____

_____

Piglet took Pooh's arm, in case Pooh was frightened.

A. A. Milne

I took your arm today because:

♡ _____

_____

_____

♥ _____

_____

_____

WE CAN ONLY LOVE A PERSON WHO EATS WHAT WE EAT.

Rigoberta Menchú

Food we both like:

♡ _____

_____

_____

♥ _____

_____

_____

Madam, I have been looking for a person who disliked gravy all my life; let us swear eternal friendship.

Reverend Sydney Smith

Food we both dislike:

♡ _____

_____

_____

♥ _____

_____

_____

A LITTLE OF WHAT YOU CALL
TOWARDS LOOKING LIKE THE

DATE: ___/___/___

My favorite outfit on you:

 _____

_____

_____

 _____

_____

_____

FRIPPERY IS VERY NECESSARY
REST OF THE WORLD. ◀ Abigail Adams

DATE: ___/___/___

My least favorite outfit on you:

♡ _____

_____

_____

♥ _____

_____

_____

DATE: ___/___/___

WHY TODAY WAS LIKE THE FIRST DAY OF A HONEYMOON:

♡ _____

_____

♥ _____

_____

DATE: ___/___/___

WHY TODAY WAS LIKE THE LAST DAY OF A VACATION:

♡ _____

_____

♥ _____

_____

Happiness consists of living each day as if it were the first day of your honeymoon and the last day of your vacation.

Leo Tolstoy

WHO LOVES ME WILL LOVE MY DOG ALSO.

St. Bernard of Clairvaux

♡ Who loves me will love my _____ also.

♥ Who loves me will love my _____ also.

DATE: __/__/__

TOGETHER DAY

{ PETS }

We spent the day today caring for a

_____.

♡ _____ ♥ _____
RATING 1–10   RATING 1–10

THE TRUE CHARM OF PEDESTRIANISM DOES NOT LIE IN THE WALKING, OR IN THE SCENERY, BUT IN THE TALKING.

Mark Twain

Our charming walk-and-talk today:

♡ _____

_____

_____

♥ _____

_____

_____

With thee conversing I forget all time,
All seasons, and their change; all
please alike.

John Milton

Our absorbing conversation today:

♡ _____

_____

_____

♥ _____

_____

_____

NOTHING WEIGHS SO HEAVY AS A SECRET.

Jean de la Fontaine

DATE: ___/___/___

A SECRET I KEEP FOR YOU:

♡ _____

_____

♥ _____

_____

DATE: ___/___/___

A SECRET YOU KEEP FOR ME:

♡ _____

_____

♥ _____

_____

I never said, "I want to be alone." I only said, "I want to be *left* alone." There is all the difference.

Greta Garbo

Why I wanted to be left alone today:

♡ _____

_____

_____

♥ _____

_____

_____

But let there be spaces in your togetherness.
And let the winds of the heavens dance between you.

Kahlil Gibran

A space in our togetherness today:

♡ _____

_____

_____

♥ _____

_____

_____

YOU COULD READ KANT BY YOURSELF, IF YOU WANTED; BUT YOU MUST SHARE A JOKE WITH SOMEONE ELSE.

Robert Louis Stevenson

A joke I shared with you today:

♡ _____

_____

_____

♥ _____

_____

_____

PERSONALITY RATING

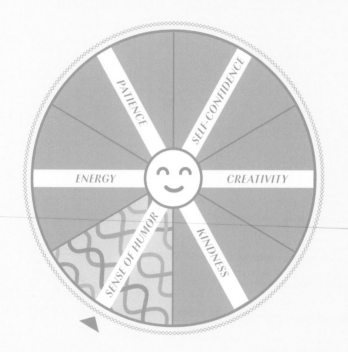

On a scale of 1 to 10, rate yourself and each other:

♡

♥

♡ _____

♥ _____

♥ _____

♡ _____

DATE: ___ / ___ / ___

MANY HANDS
MAKE LIGHT
WORK.

Greek proverb

What we accomplished together today:

♡ _____

_____

_____

♥ _____

_____

_____

DATE: ___/___/___

BURDENS SHARED ARE EASIER TO BEAR.

Jesse Jackson

A burden we shared today:

♡ _____

_____

_____

♥ _____

_____

_____

DATE: ___/___/___

WHEN I TRUSTED YOU TODAY:

♡ _____

_____

♥ _____

_____

DATE: ___/___/___

WHEN I REVERED YOU TODAY:

♡ _____

_____

♥ _____

_____

NO SOUL
IS DESOLATE
AS LONG AS
THERE IS A
HUMAN BEING
FOR WHOM
IT CAN FEEL TRUST
AND REVERENCE.

George Eliot

The sound of a kiss is not so loud as that of a cannon, but its echo lasts a great deal longer.

Oliver Wendell Holmes Sr.

The echo of our kiss today:

♡ _____

_____

_____

♥ _____

_____

_____

DATE: ___/___/___

THE SLOWEST KISS MAKES TOO MUCH HASTE.

Thomas Middleton

A kiss that made too much haste today:

♡ _____

_____

_____

♥ _____

_____

_____

DATE: ___/___/___

MEMORY LANE

My favorite memory of our first vacation together:

♡ _____

_____

_____

_____

_____

♥ _____

_____

_____

_____

_____

I have found out that there ain't no surer way to find out whether you like people or hate them than to travel with them.

Mark Twain

The trip when I found out I liked you:

♡ _____

_____

_____

♥ _____

_____

_____

Charity begins at home.

Thomas Fuller

DATE: ___/___/___

WE BEGAN THIS CHARITY AT HOME TODAY:

♡ _____

_____

♥ _____

_____

DATE: ___/___/___

WE BROUGHT THIS CHARITY TO THE WORLD TODAY:

♡ _____

_____

♥ _____

_____

THERE CAN NEVER BE ENOUGH SAID OF THE VIRTUES, THE DANGERS, THE POWERS OF A SHARED LAUGH.

Françoise Sagan

The power of our shared laugh today:

♡ _____

_____

_____

♥ _____

_____

_____

I like nonsense, it wakes up the brain cells.

Dr. Seuss

Nonsense we shared today:

♡ _____

_____

_____

♥ _____

_____

_____

The excellence of a gift lies in its appropriateness rather than in its value.

Charles Dudley Warner

The most appropriate gift you ever gave me:

♡ _____

_____

_____

♥ _____

_____

_____

DATE: ___/___/___

LOVE LETTERS

Place your stamp (♡ or ♥) on the message of love you delivered today.

When first we met we did not guess
That Love would prove so hard a master.

Robert Bridges

Why love was a hard master today:

♡ _____

_____

_____

♥ _____

_____

_____

WE'VE GOT THIS GIFT OF LOVE, BUT LOVE IS LIKE A PRECIOUS PLANT. . . . YOU'VE GOT TO KEEP WATERING IT. YOU'VE GOT TO REALLY LOOK AFTER IT AND NURTURE IT.

John Lennon

How I nurtured our love today:

♡ _____

_____

_____

♥ _____

_____

_____

DATE: ___/___/___

THE PROBLEM WE SOLVED TOGETHER TODAY:

♡ _____

_____

♥ _____

_____

DATE: ___/___/___

THE PROBLEM I COULD NOT SOLVE WITHOUT YOU TODAY:

♡ _____

_____

♥ _____

_____

There are
no problems
we cannot
solve together,
and very few
we can solve by
ourselves.

Lyndon B. Johnson

Love reckons Hours for
Months, and Days for Years:
And every little Absence is
an Age.

John Dryden

♡ You were gone for _____ today;

it felt like _____ .

♥ You were gone for _____ today;

it felt like _____ .

WHERE'ER I ROAM,
   WHATEVER REALMS TO SEE,
MY HEART UNTRAVELL'D
   FONDLY TURNS TO THEE.

Oliver Goldsmith

What I missed about you while we were apart today:

♡ _____

_____

_____

♥ _____

_____

_____

TOGETHER
DAY

{ COMMUNITY SERVICE }

The community service we did together today:

_____

♡ _____   ♥ _____
RATING 1–10   RATING 1–10

EVERYTHING BAD THAT'S EVER HAPPENED TO ME HAS TAUGHT ME COMPASSION.

Ellen DeGeneres

What taught me compassion today:

♡ _____

_____

_____

♥ _____

_____

_____

IT'S THE FRIENDS YOU CAN CALL UP AT 4 A.M. THAT MATTER.

Marlene Dietrich

How you helped when I woke you up today:

♡ _____

_____

_____

♥ _____

_____

_____

It's not so much our friends' help that helps us as the confident knowledge that they will help us.

Epicurus

I knew you would help me today when:

♡ _____

_____

_____

♥ _____

_____

_____

EVERY DAY
YOU SHOULD
REACH OUT AND
TOUCH SOMEONE.
PEOPLE LOVE A
WARM HUG, OR
JUST A FRIENDLY
PAT ON THE BACK.

Maya Angelou

DATE: ___/___/___

TODAY'S WARM HUG FROM YOU:

♡ _____

_____

♥ _____

_____

DATE: ___/___/___

TODAY'S FRIENDLY PAT ON THE BACK FROM YOU:

♡ _____

_____

♥ _____

_____

Life isn't a matter of milestones, but of moments.

Rose Kennedy

A special moment for us today:

♡ _____

_____

_____

♥ _____

_____

_____

What is this life if, full of care, We have no time to stand and stare.

W. H. Davies

When I stood and stared today:

♡ _____

_____

_____

♥ _____

_____

_____

DATE: ___/___/___

A BLUSH IS NO LANGUAGE:
WHICH MAY MEAN EITHER OF

♡ When you blush, it might mean: _____

_____

♥ When you blush, it might mean: _____

_____

DATE: ___/___/___

NLY A DUBIOUS FLAG-SIGNAL
WO CONTRADICTORIES. ◀ **George Eliot**

♡ When you blush, it might mean instead: _____

_____

♥ When you blush, it might mean instead: _____

_____

Through perils both of wind and limb, Through thick and thin she follow'd him.

Samuel Butler

You took this risk with me today:

♡ _____

_____

_____

♥ _____

_____

_____

DATE: ___/___/___

TO BE TRUSTED IS A GREATER COMPLIMENT THAN TO BE LOVED.

George Macdonald

When I trusted you today:

♡ _____

_____

_____

♥ _____

_____

_____

DATE: ___ /___ /___

A GLORIOUS MOMENT OF LOVE TODAY:

♡ _____

_____

♥ _____

_____

DATE: ___ /___ /___

A PAINFUL MOMENT OF JEALOUSY TODAY:

♡ _____

_____

♥ _____

_____

THERE IS NO GREATER GLORY THAN LOVE, NOR ANY GREATER PUNISHMENT THAN JEALOUSY.

Lope de Vega

It's a delightful thing to think of perfection; but it's vastly more amusing to talk of errors and absurdities.

Fanny Burney

An error or absurdity from my day today:

♡ _____

_____

_____

♥ _____

_____

_____

DONE IS BETTER THAN PERFECT.

Mark Zuckerberg

Something I deemed "done" today:

♡ _____

_____

_____

♥ _____

_____

_____

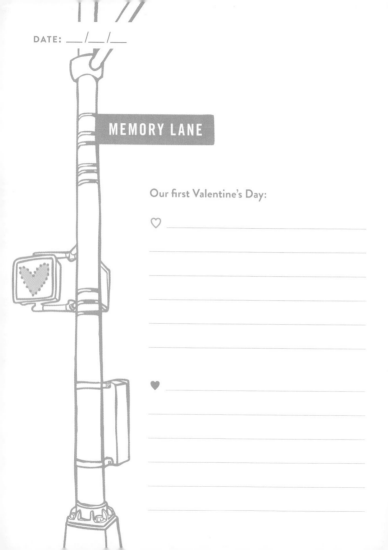

DATE: ___/___/___

MEMORY LANE

Our first Valentine's Day:

♡ _____

_____

_____

_____

_____

_____

♥ _____

_____

_____

_____

_____

_____

IT WAS ROSES, ROSES, ALL THE WAY.

Robert Browning

My favorite way we celebrate Valentine's Day:

♡ _____

_____

_____

♥ _____

_____

_____

DATE: ___/___/___

Strange to see how a good dinner and feasting reconciles everybody.

Samuel Pepys

How we reconciled after a good dinner today:

♡ _____

_____

_____

♥ _____

_____

_____

DATE: ___/___/___

SHARING FOOD WITH ANOTHER HUMAN BEING IS AN INTIMATE ACT THAT SHOULD NOT BE INDULGED IN LIGHTLY.

M. F. K. Fisher

What we shared during an intimate meal today:

♡ _____

_____

_____

♥ _____

_____

_____

*I CONFESS
MYSELF TO BE
A GREAT
ADMIRER OF
TRADITION.*

Winston Churchill

DATE: ___/___/___

A TRADITION OF OURS I ENJOY:

♡ _____

_____

♥ _____

_____

DATE: ___/___/___

A TRADITION I WANT TO START WITH YOU TODAY:

♡ _____

_____

♥ _____

_____

"The time has come," the Walrus said, "To talk of many things."

Lewis Carroll

How do you define our relationship?

♡ _____

_____

_____

♥ _____

_____

_____

DATE: ___/___/___

IT TAKES TWO TO SPEAK
THE TRUTH—ONE TO SPEAK,
AND ANOTHER TO HEAR.

Henry David Thoreau

A truth about us I heard you speak today:

♡ _____

_____

_____

♥ _____

_____

_____

FAMOUS COUPLES

Barack ♥ Michelle

How do we compare?

♡ _____

_____

_____

♥ _____

_____

_____

DATE: ___/___/___

BARACK DIDN'T PLEDGE RICHES, ONLY A LIFE THAT WOULD BE INTERESTING. ON THAT PROMISE HE DELIVERED.

Michelle Obama

How you made our life together interesting today:

♡ _____

_____

_____

♥ _____

_____

_____

DATE: ___ / ___ / ___

A SINGLE CONVERSATION ACROSS THE TABLE WITH A WISE MAN IS BETTER THAN TEN YEARS' MERE STUDY OF BOOKS.

Henry Wadsworth Longfellow

What I learned from a conversation we had today:

♡ _____

_____

_____

♥ _____

_____

_____

DATE: ___/___/___

Inject a few raisins of conversation into the tasteless dough of existence.

O. Henry

Your raisin of conversation that spiced up my bland day:

♡ _____

_____

_____

♥ _____

_____

_____

ONLY GOD, MY DEAR,
COULD LOVE YOU FOR
AND NOT YOUR

DATE: ___/___/___

My favorite hairstyle of yours:

 _____

_____

_____

_____

_____

_____

YOURSELF ALONE

YELLOW HAIR. ◀ William Butler Yeats

DATE: ___/___/___

My least favorite hairstyle of yours:

♡ _____

_____

_____

♥ _____

_____

_____

DATE: ___/___/___

A FAULT OF YOURS:

♡ _____

_____

♥ _____

_____

DATE: ___/___/___

A FAULT OF MINE THAT I SHOULD MEND:

♡ _____

_____

♥ _____

_____

TELL ME MY FAULTS, AND MEND YOUR OWN.

Benjamin Franklin

A pleasant companion on a journey is as good as a carriage.

Syrus

What I love about traveling with you:

♡ _____

_____

_____

♥ _____

_____

_____

DATE: ___/___/___

TOGETHER DAY

{ TRAVEL }

Where we traveled today:

_____

_____

♡ _____   ♥ _____

RATING 1–10   *RATING 1–10*

DATE: ___/___/___

There's no finer caress than a love letter.

Cecilia Capuzzi

Your love letter today:

♡ _____

_____

_____

♥ _____

_____

_____

The best letters of our time are precisely those that can never be published.

Virginia Woolf

An unpublishable letter from you today:

♡ _____

_____

_____

♥ _____

_____

_____

Dare to be yourself.

André Gide

DATE: ___ / ___ / ___

HOW I WAS MOST MYSELF IN PUBLIC TODAY:

♡ _____

_____

♥ _____

_____

DATE: ___ / ___ / ___

HOW I WAS MOST MYSELF WITH YOU TODAY:

♡ _____

_____

♥ _____

_____

HOBBIES OF ANY KIND ARE BORING EXCEPT TO PEOPLE WHO HAVE THE SAME HOBBY.

Dave Barry

Hobbies of yours I share:

♡ _____

_____

_____

♥ _____

_____

_____

If a man watches three televised football games in a row, he should be declared legally dead.

Erma Bombeck

A hobby of yours that drives me crazy:

♡ _____

_____

_____

♥ _____

_____

_____

I SUPPOSE IF YOU HAD TO CHOOSE JUST ONE QUALITY TO HAVE THAT WOULD BE IT: VITALITY.

John F. Kennedy

What I did with vitality today:

♡ _____

_____

_____

♥ _____

_____

_____

PERSONALITY RATING

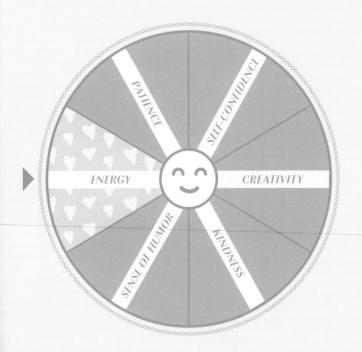

On a scale of 1 to 10, rate yourself and each other:

♡ _____

♡ _____   ♥ _____

♥ _____   ♡ _____

One of the oldest human needs is having someone to wonder where you are when you don't come home at night.

Margaret Mead

How I knew that you worried about me today:

♡ _____

_____

_____

♥ _____

_____

_____

DATE: ___/___/___

TEN O'CLOCK ... AND BACK HE'LL COME. I CAN JUST SEE HIM. WITH VINE LEAVES IN HIS HAIR. FLUSHED AND CONFIDENT.

Henrik Ibsen

How you looked to me at the end of today:

♡ _____

_____

_____

♥ _____

_____

_____

DATE: ___/___/___

HOW WE PROTECTED EACH OTHER'S SOLITUDE TODAY:

♡ _____

_____

♥ _____

_____

DATE: ___/___/___

HOW WE TOUCHED AND GREETED EACH OTHER
FROM OUR SOLITUDES TODAY:

♡ _____

_____

♥ _____

_____

LOVE CONSISTS IN THIS, THAT TWO SOLITUDES PROTECT AND TOUCH AND GREET EACH OTHER.

Rainer Maria Rilke

DATE: ___/___/___

*She has made me in
love with a cold climate,
and frost and snow,
with a northern moonlight.*

Robert Southey

Before I met you, I never liked:

♡ _____

_____

_____

♥ _____

_____

_____

DATE: ___/___/___

LOVE TEACHES EVEN ASSES TO DANCE.

French proverb

Before I met you, I never tried:

♡ _____

_____

_____

♥ _____

_____

_____

DATE: ___/___/___

MEMORY LANE

Our first crisis together:

♡ _____

_____

_____

_____

_____

_____

♥ _____

_____

_____

_____

_____

_____

_____

THE GOOD ARE BETTER MADE BY ILL, AS ODOURS CRUSHED ARE SWEETER STILL.

Samuel Rogers

How you rose to a crisis today:

♡ _____

_____

_____

♥ _____

_____

_____

WHEN A MATCH
HAS EQUAL PARTNERS
THEN I FEAR NOT.

Aeschylus

DATE: ___/___/___

A WAY IN WHICH WE ARE EQUAL:

♡ _____

_____

♥ _____

_____

DATE: ___/___/___

A WAY IN WHICH WE ARE UNEQUAL:

♡ _____

_____

♥ _____

_____

DATE: ___/___/___

I've met a lot of hardboiled eggs in my time, but you—you're twenty minutes.

Ace in the Hole

♡ You are as tough as a _____ -minute hardboiled egg.

♥ You are as tough as a _____ -minute hardboiled egg.

I'M NOT HARD—
I'M FRIGHTFULLY
SOFT. BUT I WILL
NOT BE HOUNDED.

Margaret Thatcher

What I would not be hounded about today:

♡ _____

_____

_____

♥ _____

_____

_____

The most delicious pleasure is to cause that of other people.

La Bruyère

My most delicious pleasure today was to please you by:

♡ _____

_____

_____

♥ _____

_____

_____

LOVE LETTERS

Place your stamp (♡ or ♥) on the message of love you delivered today.

flowers

a scented candle

tickets to a movie, show, or sporting event

a homemade gift

a love note in a secret spot

a tasty treat or homemade meal

a warm bubble bath

other

_____

There are formalities between the closest of friends.

Japanese proverb

A formality we observe between us:

♡ _____

_____

_____

♥ _____

_____

_____

DATE: ___/___/___

FRIENDS SHARE ALL THINGS.

Pythagoras

What we shared today:

♡ _____

_____

_____

♥ _____

_____

_____

DATE: ___/___/___

I LOVED THIS TRUTH YOU TOLD ME TODAY:

♡ _____

_____

♥ _____

_____

DATE: ___/___/___

I PARDONED THIS ERROR OF YOURS TODAY:

♡ _____

_____

♥ _____

_____

LOVE TRUTH, BUT PARDON ERROR.

Voltaire

{ ALVY }

A relationship, I think, is, is like a shark, you know, it has to constantly move forward or it dies.

Annie Hall

How our relationship moved forward today:

♡ _____

_____

_____

♥ _____

_____

_____

Love doesn't just sit there, like a stone, it has to be made, like bread; remade all the time, made new.

Ursula K. Le Guin

How I kneaded our relationship today:

♡ _____

_____

_____

♥ _____

_____

_____

DATE: ___/___/___

TOGETHER
DAY

{ GAMES }

The game we played together today:

_____

♡ _____   ♥ _____

RATING 1–10   *RATING 1–10*

DATE: ___/___/___

LIFE'S TOO SHORT FOR CHESS.

Henry James Byron

♡ My life's long enough for _____ .

♥ My life's long enough for _____ .

THINK THAT DAY LOST WHOSE LOW DESCENDING SUN VIEWS FROM THY HAND NO NOBLE ACTION DONE.

Jacob Bobart

My noble action today:

♡ _____

_____

♥ _____

_____

_____

*So many worlds, so
    much to do,
So little done, such
    things to be.*

Alfred, Lord Tennyson

What we got done together today:

♡ _____

_____

_____

♥ _____

_____

_____

COUPLES
ARE WHOLES
AND NOT WHOLES,
WHAT AGREES
DISAGREES,
THE CONCORDANT
IS DISCORDANT.

Heraclitus

DATE: ___/___/___

HOW WE WERE WHOLE TODAY:

♡ _____

_____

♥ _____

_____

DATE: ___/___/___

HOW WE WERE NOT WHOLE TODAY:

♡ _____

_____

♥ _____

_____

DATE: ___/___/___

I HAVE NEVER KNOWN ANYONE WORTH A DAMN WHO WASN'T IRASCIBLE.

Ezra Pound

When you were irascible today:

♡ _____

_____

_____

♥ _____

_____

_____

The only people for me are the mad ones, the ones who are mad to live, mad to talk, mad to be saved, desirous of everything at the same time.

Jack Kerouac

The only people for me are:

♡ _____

_____

_____

_____

♥ _____

_____

_____

THAT MAN'S SILENCE IS

♡ What your silence in social situations means: _____

_____

♥ What your silence in social situations means: _____

_____

DATE: ___/___/___

VONDERFUL TO LISTEN TO.

◀ *Thomas Hardy*

♡ What your silence with me alone means: _____

_____

♥ What your silence with me alone means: _____

_____

CHANGE IS NOT MADE WITHOUT INCONVENIENCE, EVEN FROM WORSE TO BETTER.

Richard Hooker

An inconvenient change we made for the better:

♡ _____

_____

_____

♥ _____

_____

_____

We have met too late. You are too old for me to have any effect on you.

James Joyce

We met in time for you to have this effect on me:

♡ _____

_____

_____

_____

♥ _____

_____

_____

DATE: ___ /___ /___

HOW OUR RELATIONSHIP KEEPS ME HAPPIER:

♡ _____

_____

♥ _____

_____

DATE: ___ /___ /___

HOW OUR RELATIONSHIP KEEPS ME HEALTHIER:

♡ _____

_____

♥ _____

_____

The clearest
message that we
get . . . is this:
Good relationships
keep us happier
and healthier.

Study of Adult Development, Harvard Medical School

A LITTLE OF
WHAT YOU FANCY
DOES YOU GOOD.

Frank W. Leigh and George Arthurs

What I fancied today:

♡ _____

_____

_____

♥ _____

_____

_____

Who can enjoy alone?
Or all enjoying, what
contentment find?

John Milton

What we enjoyed together today:

♡ _____

_____

_____

♥ _____

_____

_____

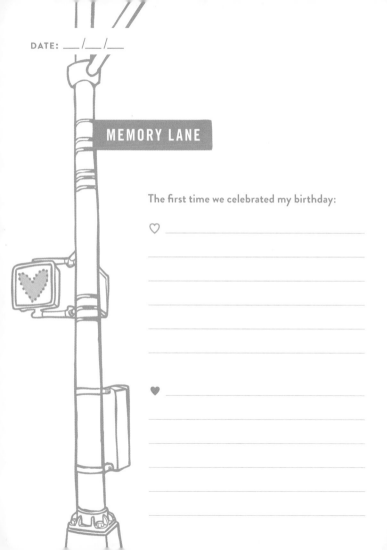

DATE: ___/___/___

MEMORY LANE

The first time we celebrated my birthday:

♡ _____

_____

_____

_____

_____

_____

♥ _____

_____

_____

_____

_____

_____

DATE: __/__/__

YOUR BIRTH-DAY, AS MY OWN,
TO ME IS DEAR. . . .
BUT YOURS GIVES MOST; FOR
MINE DID ONLY LEND
ME TO THE WORLD; YOURS
GAVE TO ME A FRIEND.

Martial

What I like best about celebrating your birthday:

♡ _____

_____

_____

♥ _____

_____

_____

WE SOMETIMES THINK THAT WE HATE FLATTERY, BUT WE ONLY HATE THE MANNER IN WHICH IT IS DONE.

François de La Rochefoucauld

How you compliment me:

♡ _____

_____

_____

♥ _____

_____

I can live for two months on a good compliment.

Mark Twain

Thank you for this compliment today:

♡ _____

_____

_____

♥ _____

_____

_____

Reality, as usual, beats fiction out of sight.

Joseph Conrad

DATE: ___/___/___

SOMETHING INCREDIBLE ABOUT US AS A COUPLE:

♡ _____

_____

♥ _____

_____

DATE: ___/___/___

SOMETHING CRAZY THAT HAPPENED TODAY:

♡ _____

_____

♥ _____

_____

Love is that condition in which the happiness of another person is essential to your own.

Robert A. Heinlein

This happiness of yours made me happy today:

♡ _____

_____

_____

♥ _____

_____

_____

LOVE SEEKETH NOT ITSELF TO PLEASE,

NOR FOR ITSELF HATH ANY CARE,

BUT FOR ANOTHER GIVES ITS EASE,

AND BUILDS A HEAVEN IN HELL'S DESPAIR.

William Blake

How you built a heaven in my despair today:

♡ _____

_____

_____

♥ _____

_____

_____

FAMOUS COUPLES

—

Kate

♥

William

How do we compare?

♡ _____

_____

_____

♥ _____

_____

_____

We take the mickey out of each other a lot, and she's got plenty of habits that make me laugh that I tease her about.

Prince William

A habit you teased me about today:

♡ _____

_____

_____

♥ _____

_____

_____

Whether you're a man or a woman, the fascination resides in finding out that we're alike.

Marguerite Duras

How we are alike:

♡ _____

_____

_____

♥ _____

_____

_____

DATE: ___/___/___

OPPOSITES ATTRACT.

▲
American proverb
▼

How we are opposite:

♡ _____

_____

_____

♥ _____

_____

_____

"WHATEVER" IS THE MOST ___ IN CASUAL CONVERSATION FOR ___

DATE: ___/___/___

My favorite expression of yours:

 _____

_____

_____

 _____

_____

_____

ANNOYING WORD OR PHRASE
THE EIGHTH YEAR RUNNING.

◀ Marist Institute for Public Opinion, 2016

DATE: ___/___/___

My least favorite expression of yours:

♡ _____

_____

_____

♥ _____

_____

_____

DATE: ___ / ___ / ___

THIS EVENT WITH THE HEART CAUSED ME GREAT JOY:

♡ _____

_____

♥ _____

_____

DATE: ___ / ___ / ___

THIS EVENT WITH THE HEART CAUSED ME GREAT SADNESS:

♡ _____

_____

♥ _____

_____

THERE ARE NO LITTLE EVENTS WITH THE HEART.... IT PLACES IN THE SAME SCALES THE FALL OF AN EMPIRE OF FOURTEEN YEARS AND THE DROPPING OF A WOMAN'S GLOVE, AND ALMOST ALWAYS THE GLOVE WEIGHS MORE THAN THE EMPIRE.

Honoré de Balzac

NOTHING HAPPENS, AND NOTHING HAPPENS, AND THEN EVERYTHING HAPPENS.

Fay Weldon

Everything that happened on this nothing day:

♡ _____

_____

_____

♥ _____

_____

_____

DATE: ___/___/___

TOGETHER
DAY

{ DOING NOTHING }

What we didn't do today:

_____

♡ _____
RATING 1–10

♥ _____
RATING 1–10

DATE: ___/___/___

SOMEONE SAID THAT GOD GAVE US MEMORY SO THAT WE MIGHT HAVE ROSES IN DECEMBER.

J. M. Barrie

A rose from today I will save for December:

♡ _____

_____

_____

♥ _____

_____

_____

Bliss in possession will not last;
Remember'd joys are never past.

James F. Montgomery

Today I remembered this past joy:

♡ _____

_____

_____

♥ _____

_____

_____

The
Muses
love
the
Morning.

Thomas Fuller

DATE: ___/___/___

MY MUSES LOVED THIS TIME TODAY:

♡ _____

_____

♥ _____

_____

DATE: ___/___/___

MY MUSES LOVED THIS PLACE TODAY:

♡ _____

_____

♥ _____

_____

LIFE IS TOO SHORT TO STUFF A MUSHROOM.

Shirley Conran

Life is not too short to do this for you:

♡ _____

_____

_____

♥ _____

_____

_____

DATE: ___/___/___

Good food is always a trouble and its preparation should be regarded as a labour of love.

Elizabeth David

My labor of love in the kitchen today:

♡ _____

_____

_____

♥ _____

_____

_____

With time and patience the mulberry leaf becomes a silk gown.

Chinese proverb

How patience paid off today:

♡ _____

_____

_____

♥ _____

_____

_____

DATE: ___/___/___

PERSONALITY RATING

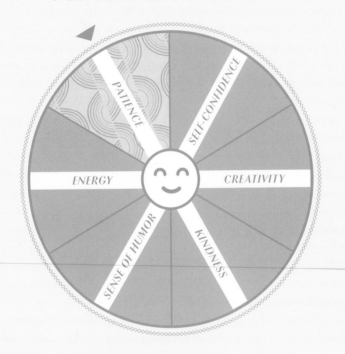

On a scale of 1 to 10, rate yourself and each other:

♡ _____   ♥ _____

♡ _____   ♥ _____

♥ _____   ♡ _____

A lonely man is a lonesome thing, a stone, a bone, a stick, a receptacle for Gilbey's gin, a stooped figure sitting at the edge of a hotel bed, heaving copious sighs like the autumn wind.

John Cheever

What my life was like before there was us:

♡ _____

_____

_____

♥ _____

_____

_____

Please fence me in baby the world's too big out here and I don't like it without you.

Humphrey Bogart, telegram

Please fence me in because:

♡ _____

_____

_____

♥ _____

_____

_____

DATE: ___/___/___

WHAT MY LIFE WAS BASED ON DOING TODAY:

♡ _____

_____

♥ _____

_____

DATE: ___/___/___

WHAT MY LIFE WAS BASED ON BEING TODAY:

♡ _____

_____

♥ _____

_____

LIVES BASED
ON HAVING
ARE LESS FREE
THAN LIVES
BASED EITHER
ON DOING
OR ON BEING.

William James

DATE: ___/___/___

TWO THINGS A MAN CANNOT HIDE: THAT HE IS DRUNK, AND THAT HE IS IN LOVE.

Antiphanes

How my friends could tell I was in love with you:

♡ _____

_____

_____

♥ _____

_____

_____

DATE: ___/___/___

LOVE MAKES FOOLS OF ALL OF US, BIG AND LITTLE.

William Makepeace Thackeray

How love made a fool of me today:

♡ _____

_____

_____

♥ _____

_____

_____

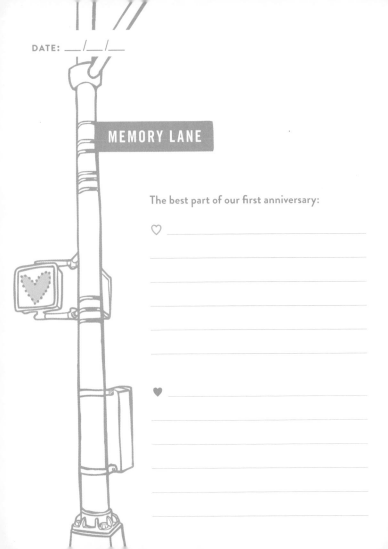

DATE: ___/___/___

MEMORY LANE

The best part of our first anniversary:

♡ _____

_____

_____

_____

_____

♥ _____

_____

_____

_____

_____

_____

DATE: ___/___/___

The holiest of all holidays are those
Kept by ourselves in silence and apart;
The secret anniversaries of the heart.

Henry Wadsworth Longfellow

A secret anniversary we celebrated today:

♡ _____

_____

_____

♥ _____

_____

_____

WHEN WRITTEN
IN CHINESE
THE WORD CRISIS
IS COMPOSED OF
TWO CHARACTERS.
ONE REPRESENTS
DANGER
AND THE OTHER
REPRESENTS
OPPORTUNITY.

John F. Kennedy

DATE: __/__/__

THE DANGER IN OUR CRISIS TODAY:

♡ _____

_____

♥ _____

_____

DATE: __/__/__

THE OPPORTUNITY IN OUR CRISIS TODAY:

♡ _____

_____

♥ _____

_____

DATE: ___/___/___

BUT I HAVE PROMISES TO KEEP, AND MILES TO GO BEFORE I SLEEP.

Robert Frost

A promise you kept today:

♡ _____

_____

_____

♥ _____

_____

_____

DATE: __/__/__

A promise made is a debt unpaid.

Robert W. Service

A promise you have yet to keep:

♡ _____

_____

_____

♥ _____

_____

_____

The key to a woman's heart is an unexpected gift at an unexpected time.

Mike Rich

A gift you gave me that unlocked my heart:

♡ _____

_____

_____

♥ _____

_____

_____

DATE: ___/___/___

LOVE LETTERS

Place your stamp (♡ or ♥) on the message of love you delivered today.

flowers

a scented candle

tickets to a movie, show, or sporting event

a homemade gift

a love note in a secret spot

a tasty treat or homemade meal

a warm bubble bath

other
_____

DATE: ___/___/___

SHE FELT THE NATURAL TIES OF AFFINITY RATHER THAN THE CONVENTIONAL BLIND TIES OF THE BLOOD.

Nadine Gordimer

Our natural ties of affinity:

♡ _____

_____

_____

♥ _____

_____

_____

DATE: ___/___/___

*Ah, how much I like you,
how well we get on, when
you're asleep and I'm
awake.*

Colette

When we get along best:

♡ _____

_____

_____

♥ _____

_____

_____

DATE: ___/___/___

WHAT I CAN DO WITHOUT:

♡ _____

_____

♥ _____

_____

DATE: ___/___/___

WHAT I CANNOT DO WITHOUT:

♡ _____

_____

♥ _____

_____

HOW MANY MANY THINGS I CAN DO WITHOUT!

Socrates

Nothing is so contagious as example.

François de La Rochefoucauld

Your example today has inspired me to:

♡ _____

_____

_____

♥ _____

_____

_____

Setting too good an Example is a Kind of Slander seldom forgiven.

Benjamin Franklin

I felt bad that I couldn't live up to your example today:

♡ _____

_____

_____

♥ _____

_____

_____

TOGETHER DAY

{ READING }

What we read today:

_____

♡ _____   ♥ _____

RATING 1–10   *RATING 1–10*

The pleasure of all reading is doubled when one lives with another who shares the same books.

Katherine Mansfield

My favorite book we shared:

♡ _____

_____

_____

♥ _____

_____

_____

THE MEETING OF TWO PERSONALITIES IS LIKE THE CONTACT OF TWO CHEMICAL SUBSTANCES: IF THERE IS ANY REACTION, BOTH ARE TRANSFORMED.

Carl Gustav Jung

How I was transformed by meeting you:

♡ _____

_____

_____

♥ _____

_____

_____

DATE: ___/___/___

RELATIONSHIP *IS* A PERVADING AND CHANGING MYSTERY.

Eudora Welty

How our relationship has changed over time:

♡ _____

_____

_____

♥ _____

_____

_____

THINK ONLY OF THE PAST AS ITS REMEMBRANCE GIVES YOU PLEASURE.

Jane Austen

DATE: ___/___/___

AN EVENT FROM MY LIFE I WANT TO REMEMBER:

♡ _____

_____

♥ _____

_____

DATE: ___/___/___

AN EVENT FROM OUR LIFE TOGETHER I WANT TO REMEMBER:

♡ _____

_____

♥ _____

_____

DATE: ___/___/___

AT THIS EVERY LADY DREW UP
PRONOUNCE THE LETTER P.

♡ When you do this with your mouth: _____

　　　　it means: _____

♥ When you do this with your mouth: _____

　　　　it means: _____

DATE: ___/___/___

HER MOUTH AS IF GOING TO

◀ Oliver Goldsmith

♡ When you get this expression on your face: _____

it means: _____

♥ When you get this expression on your face: _____

it means: _____

In love,
one and one
are one.

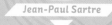

Jean-Paul Sartre

Complete this equation together:

 + 🖤 =